Building History
TUDOR THEATER

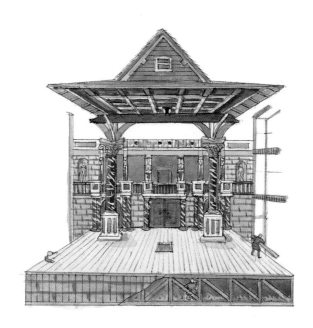

Gillian Clements

SEA-TO-SEA

Mankato Collingwood London

This edition first published in 2009 by Sea-to-Sea Publications
Distributed by Black Rabbit Books
P.O. Box 3263
Mankato, Minnesota 56002

Printed in China

Library of Congress Cataloging-in-Publication Data:

Clements, Gillian.
  Tudor theatre / Gillian Clements.
      p. cm. -- (Building history)
  Includes index.
  Summary: "Describes London theaters in the 1500s and 1600s, built by Queen Elizabeth I and King James I,
including how they were built and what kind of plays were performed"--Provided by publisher.
  ISBN 978-1-59771-147-0
  1. Theater--England--London--History--16th century--Juvenile literature. 2. Theater--England--London--History-
-17th century--Juvenile literature. 3. Theaters--England--London--History--16th century--Juvenile literature. 4.
Theaters--England--London--History--17th century--Juvenile literature. I. Title.
  PN2596.L6C53 2009
  792.0942'09031--dc22
                              2008004580

9 8 7 6 5 4 3 2

Published by arrangement with the
Watts Publishing Group Ltd, London.

Editors: Rachel Cooke and Sally Luck
Art Director: Jonathan Hair
Consultant: Dr. Catherine Alexander,
The Shakespeare Institute
(University of Birmingham)

Contents

What is a Tudor theater?

Toward the end of the 1500s, when the Tudor Queen Elizabeth I was on the throne, some extraordinary new theaters were built in London. Everyone flocked to see the exciting new plays.

What other entertainments were there?

There were already many types of entertainment in Tudor times. People could see bear-baiting and bloody executions, church mystery plays, and royal processions.

What was the Renaissance?

At this time people were interested in the Classical culture of ancient Greece and Rome and the period became known as the Renaissance (meaning rebirth). During the Renaissance many new scientific and artistic ideas were developed. The new plays performed in Tudor theaters were part of the Renaissance.

How did theaters develop ?

Greek theater,
5th century B.C.E.

Roman theater,
1st century B.C.E.

Roman amphitheater,
c. 80 B.C.E.

Who were the theaters for?

All kinds of people visited London's new theaters, from the very poor to the very rich. When a flag was flown over the theater to announce the latest play, crowds of people crossed over the Thames River to enjoy the show. Just one penny bought the cheapest ticket, and nearly everyone could afford that.

There were many outstanding people in Queen Elizabeth's kingdom, but perhaps the brightest was the playwright William Shakespeare. His plays are just as popular today as they were 400 years ago.

Where were the theaters built?

For a long time, people in cities like Coventry, Chester, and York had been able to see religious mystery plays. These were put on by local craft unions called guilds and were performed on temporary stages. However, it was businessmen who built the new Tudor theaters. And, as London was the home of business, it became the home of the Tudor theaters too.

Queen Elizabeth I and King James I ▷

When were the theaters built?

Most of these theaters were built between the late 1500s and the early 1600s, during the reigns of Queen Elizabeth I and King James I. The theaters built during Elizabeth's reign are often known as Elizabethan theaters and those built in King James's reign are known as Jacobean theaters (after the Latin word for James). This book is about both Elizabethan and Jacobean theaters.

mystery plays, 13th century

traveling players, 14th century

inn yard theater, 16th century

Tudor theater, 1570s

Jacobean theater, 1600s

Who were the Tudors?

The Tudors were the royal family who ruled England and Wales from 1485 to 1603. During this time, many changes took place and the country became richer than ever before.

Royalty

The Tudor kings and queens began in 1485 with Henry VII. The best known are Henry VIII (1509-47) and his daughter Elizabeth I (1558-1603). They were both very powerful and intelligent.

Nobles and clergy

The nobles were important families who owned a lot of land. They spent time at Court with the royal family and dressed fancy clothes to show off their wealth. The clergy—bishops and priests—also had a lot of power in Tudor times.

Queen Elizabeth was an unusually well educated lady. In Tudor times, most women did not have the privilege of an education. Elizabeth loved the arts and she wrote her own poems, sonnets, and prayers.

Merchants and explorers

England was a rich trading country in Tudor times. Merchants sold many English goods abroad, especially wool. Explorers discovered new countries to trade with. Sea captain Richard Chancellor began trade with Russia, while Francis Drake claimed land in America, as he sailed around the world.

Shopkeepers and craftsmen

Shopkeepers and craftsmen made a lot of money in England's towns and cities. Craftsmen from trades, such as book publishing, silk weaving, and goldsmithing, belonged to businesses and craft unions. These unions were known as guilds and the members of these guilds elected the town mayors.

Yeomen farmers

Yeomen farmers owned small plots of land in the country. Their main crops were wheat, barley, and rye and they had gardens for fruit, vegetables, herbs, and beehives. They also raised animals such as sheep, cows, goats, and pigs.

Laborers and beggars

Laborers and beggars were at the bottom of English society. When yeomen farmers closed fields for sheep-grazing, they threw laborers off their land. Thousands of them were forced to roam the country looking for work. Many soldiers became beggars, too. After years of war there was peace, and thousands lost their jobs. Those strong enough to work became known as "sturdy beggars."

Why build a theater?

James Burbage built the first theater in London, in 1576. It was called the Theater. There were already many types of entertainment in London, but Burbage believed that a permanent theater would be a very profitable business.

Mystery plays were still performed in some cities. These were religious plays that told Bible stories.

The Queen paid for fancy masques to take place in her palaces at Christmas and New Year. She and her courtiers took part, wearing wonderful, expensive costumes.

City pageants were organized by guilds. A series of dramatic scenes telling stories connected to the guild or local history were performed during the procession.

During royal processions the Queen was carried though London. Knights of the Garter walked in front carrying the ceremonial Sword of State.

For lively entertainment, there were fencing displays, in halls or public areas outside. These often attracted huge crowds.

Everything about Tudor London was theatrical. People dressed up in fine costumes and uniforms to take part in the many public ceremonies. Even grisly public executions and bear-baiting were very dramatic.

Those wanting peaceful entertainment could listen to outdoor sermons at St. Paul's Cross.

There were special circular arenas at Bankside, for cock-fighting and bear-baiting. Londoners flocked to these arenas to watch cockerels fight to the death, or to see dogs attack an angry bull or a bear.

Public executions were a big event. Traitors were often beheaded at the Tower of London. Their boiled heads were then crowned with ivy and put on spikes at the entrance to London Bridge.

Did people go to the theater?

Plays were performed by traveling players (actors) in public areas. There were no permanent theaters until Burbage built the Theater in 1576. The idea proved so successful it was soon copied by others.

Why did the permanent theaters work so well?

The new theaters provided a settled base for groups of writers and actors. With time and space to rehearse, these groups, known as companies, became more and more professional. Popular plays attracted crowds of 2,000 to 3,000, and so theaters like the Rose (built 1587) and the Globe (built 1599) made lots of money. With this money, the companies bought more plays, costumes, and props so they could put on even more shows.

the Globe theater, 1599

11

Where were the theaters built?

Tudor theaters were built in London. During Elizabeth I's reign, many people had moved there from other parts of England and from abroad. It was a dirty, noisy, energetic place, that spilled beyond its city walls. Theater was the ideal entertainment for this exciting city.

Travelers sharing ideas on the latest art techniques

Why was London so important?
Tudor London was a successful trading port. Many ships set sail from London on voyages of exploration around the world. As these ships left, others came in bringing travelers from Europe. These travelers shared their knowledge of the latest Renaissance ideas such as the art and architecture in Italian cities. London became a "melting pot" of new ideas.

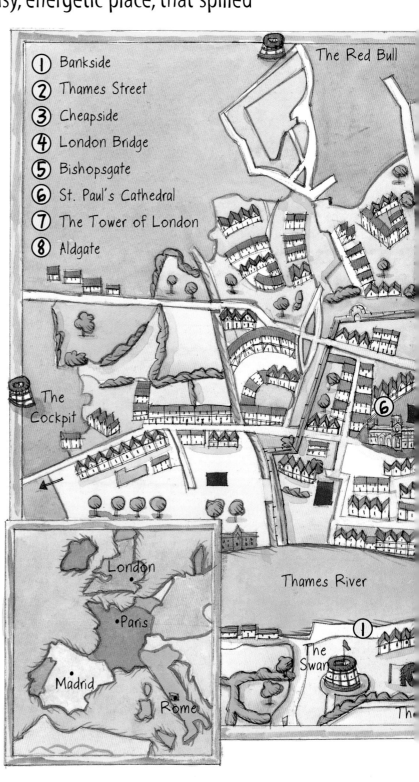

- ① Bankside
- ② Thames Street
- ③ Cheapside
- ④ London Bridge
- ⑤ Bishopsgate
- ⑥ St. Paul's Cathedral
- ⑦ The Tower of London
- ⑧ Aldgate

The Red Bull

The Cockpit

London

Paris

Madrid

Rome

Thames River

The Swan

Where were the theaters in London?

London's Lord Mayor hated theaters because of the "dangerous and ungodly" content of the plays. He also hated the large crowds they attracted. There was too much street traffic and, inside the theaters, drunken fights often broke out. The Mayor tried to ban theaters from the city center. As a result, new theaters were built outside London's walls, both north and south of the Thames River.

the city of London, (the red area) on the Thames River

The Fortune

The Theater

The Curtain

⑤

⑧

②

④

The Globe

⑦

These theaters really are a nuisance!

the Lord Mayor

The Lord Mayor could not ban theater completely because the Queen loved it. When a popular play was on in town, she commanded the actors to transport their props and costumes to her palace and perform for her there.

Who built the theaters?

The leading theater men had to be clever businessmen too. The theaters could make big profits…but first they had to be built. This required a lot of money.

Who were the leading theater men?

James Burbage, his son Richard, and their rival Philip Henslowe, were the leading theater men in London. Their jobs involved spending a lot of money. They had to buy or rent land, buy the materials for building the theater, and then pay laborers to do the construction work.

When the landlord of Burbage's theater in Shoreditch refused to allow him to stay, Burbage and 12 workmen took it down in the dead of night, carried the wood across the river and used it to build the Globe.

How did the actors form companies?

Each theater had its own company of actors. Traveling players had a reputation for being "rogues and vagabonds," so laws were needed to give the actors protection. The company at the Rose were given protection by the Lord Admiral and became known as the Lord Admiral's Men. Burbage's company at the Globe became the Lord Chamberlain's Men.

Which craftsmen built the Tudor theaters?

Carpenters

Carpenters built the Tudor theaters around a strong timber frame, usually made from oak. It was the same technique used for houses.

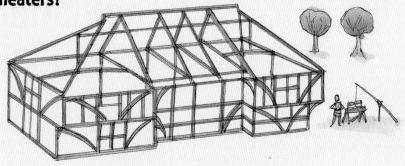

Plasterers

Plasterers also used the same technique for theaters as for houses. They filled in the gaps between the timber-framing. The outside walls were very plain but the plasterwork was often highly ornate inside.

Thatchers

Thatchers used reeds to roof Tudor houses and theaters. It was a cheap material, but could easily catch fire. The first Globe burned down in 1613, when sparks from a stage cannon landed on the thatch.

Wood carvers

These craftsmen were used to making Classical-style church monuments or screens in great houses. They now used these skills to decorate the theaters' stage area.

Painters

The best painters in England painted church tombs and ceilings in grand houses. They used these skills for painting the starry "heavens" over the stage. They painted oak pillars to make them look just like marble.

How did they build the theaters?

Building a theater was a complex operation. It was put together in many different stages and involved the work of skilled builders and craftsmen.

Foundation trenches

Laborers began the building work by digging foundation trenches. These were filled with crushed chalk or a limestone mixture called "clunch" to form a firm base. A low brick wall was then built onto this base and the timber frame was placed on top of it.

The timber frame

The beams of the timber frame were held in place with wooden pegs. Once the frame was built, stair towers were added. Wooden strips called "laths" and "staves" were placed between the timber frames to provide a support for the plastering.

Plastering

Builders filled the timber framed walls with woven wooden "wattle," which was then covered with plaster. The plaster was made by mixing lime, sand, and horse or cow hair together.

a trapdoor

the tiring-house

the galleries

the yard

the stage

Inside the theater there was a lot of carpentry to do, beginning with the galleries. These held the audience's seats. There were three tiers and each tier had three or four rows of seats. Even in heavy rain, the audience in all three tiers of the gallery would stay dry under the reed-thatched roof.

The yard was the roughest place to watch the play, and the cheapest. The floor had to be tough because as many as a thousand people might stand at each performance. It was made from sand, ash, and hazelnut shells.

▲ theater gallery

The tiring-house was the changing room where the actors put on their costumes. It was a timber-framed building at the back of the stage, and was made up of several parts. The "hut" and the "heavens," held up by pillars, were over the stage. Behind the acting area there were doors and an alcove where actors could enter and exit. There was a balcony too, for seating or for actors and musicians. The tiring-house was very grand with elaborate painting and carving.

the hut

the heavens

The hut and the heavens were used for storing costumes, props, and stage scenery, including cannons for battle scenes. A rope winch helped create important special effects. Actors dressed as gods were lowered through a trapdoor in the heavens to astonish the audience.

The stage was raised 5 feet (1.5 meters) above the ground, at face level for the audience standing in the yard. Like the heavens, it had a trapdoor for actors to make surprise entrances as if from hell or from a grave.

Who put on the plays?

Theater companies were made up of senior shareholders, actors, and boy apprentices. The whole company worked together to put on the plays, meeting at the theater every day to rehearse new parts.

Who were the actors?

The Lord Chamberlain's Men had some of England's greatest actors. Burbage was their biggest star. Their rivals were the Lord Admiral's Men and their star was Edward Alleyn. He played *Doctor Faustus* in Marlowe's play about a man who sells his soul to the devil. He was so believable that people thought there was a real devil on stage.

Who were the boy apprentices?

Women and girls did not perform in public theaters in Tudor times. Female parts were played by boy apprentices who were dressed in skirts, wigs, and makeup to look the part.

Tudor plays often included fools or clowns. They were audience favorites. William Kemp was famous for playing fools. When he left his company in 1600, he danced all the way from London to Norwich.

Richard Henslowe

William Shakespeare

Richard Burbage

a boy apprentice

William Kemp

▲ some members of the Lord Chamberlain's Men

Who were the playwrights?

Shakespeare was a successful playwright and, with the help of his patron, he became very rich. Other playwrights weren't as fortunate or talented. They were paid very little for each play. Ben Jonson and Thomas Dekker received just £8 for their play *Page of Plymouth*.

Christopher Marlowe (1564–93)

Marlowe was the son of a Canterbury shoemaker. He wrote many famous plays including *Edward II, The Jew of Malta, Doctor Faustus,* and *Tamburlaine.* His death was as dramatic as his plays. In 1593 someone stabbed him in the eye at an inn, in London.

William Shakespeare (1564–1616)

Shakespeare was the son of a Stratford glover. As a young man he traveled to London, joined a company of actors, and began writing plays and poems. He invested in the Globe and the profits made him rich. He died in 1616, at the age of 52.

Ben Jonson (1574–1637)

Jonson was a friend and rival of William Shakespeare. He was educated in Classical history and became well known for writing special entertainments for James I. Jonson also wrote powerful comedies like *Volpone* and *The Alchemist.*

Edward Alleyn

▲ *some members of the Lord Admiral's Men.*

What plays did they put on?

The theaters had to make a good profit, so any plays that were not a "hit" were axed after just a few performances. The crowds enjoyed all sorts of plays, from tragedies through to comedies and romances.

Comedy—*As You Like It* by Shakespeare

Hamlet was one of the most popular plays. It was advertised as having been "*divers times acted by his Highness' servants in the City of London, as also in the two Universities of Cambridge and Oxford, and elsewhere.*"

What made a play popular?

Tudor times were sometimes violent and dangerous. There were plots against the Queen, grisly executions, and wars against countries like Holland and Spain. In these troubled and tragic times, people loved the theater—and the funny, tragic, gory, and magical plays they saw there. Clever playwrights, like Shakespeare and Marlowe, wrote about the frightening side of Tudor life, but they also created the comedy and magic which helped people forget their troubles and cares.

Tragedy—*Othello* by Shakespeare

Gory—*Hamlet* by Shakespeare

Magic *Dr. Faustus* by Marlowe

A MIDSUMMER NIGHT'S DREAM

Bottom
Puck
Quince
Snug
Snout
Lion
Flute
Dog
Theseus Duke of Athens
Egeus and Philostrate
the Lovers
Helena Hermia Lysander Demetrius
Titania and Oberon

A MIDSUMMER NIGHT'S DREAM
a magnificent new play by Mr. Will Shakespeare, a story of magic and tangled love

▶ an advertising playbill

What happened before the plays began?

During the summer, there was a performance at the Globe every afternoon. Advertising bills were handed out around London and, on the afternoon of the performance, a flag was flown over the theater to announce the start of the play. When they saw the flag, play-goers hurried to the Globe, scrambling across London Bridge (the only bridge over the Thames River), or taking water-taxis called wherries. The entrance fee was paid to the doorman who stood by the theater stairs.

PRICES

1d (one penny)—to stand in the yard as a groundling

2d—a gallery seat

3d—a gallery seat AND a cushion

6d—a balcony seat behind the stage, or in the Lord's gallery seats near the stage

Were any of the plays censored?

The Lord Chamberlain was allowed to censor or cancel plays if he thought the content was too dangerous. This followed an event in 1601 when the Earl of Essex paid the company 40 shillings to put on Shakespeare's play *Richard II*. It was all about a king's murder. The Earl hoped the play would encourage people to overthrow Queen Elizabeth.

▶ At 2 o'clock a trumpeter sounded a fanfare from the tiring-house hut. The play had begun.

How did they stage a play?

Today at the Globe, the Lord Chamberlain's Men are putting on *A Midsummer Night's Dream*. The company have been rehearsing for weeks and the play is expected to be a huge success.

What happened behind the scenes?

The actors dressed or "attired" behind the scenes in the tiring-house. They were helped by dressers called "tiremen." A bookkeeper would also stay behind the scenes. He helped the actors remember their lines. He even nailed a "platt" (a piece of paper explaining the plot) onto a door to help remind them of the running order.

What special effects were used?

The winch above the heavens would have been useful in the production of *A Midsummer Night's Dream*. When the character called Puck is supposed to fly or "girdle the Earth in forty seconds" he could have been lowered over the stage by a rope. A second trapdoor in the stage allowed characters like the fairies to appear as if by magic.

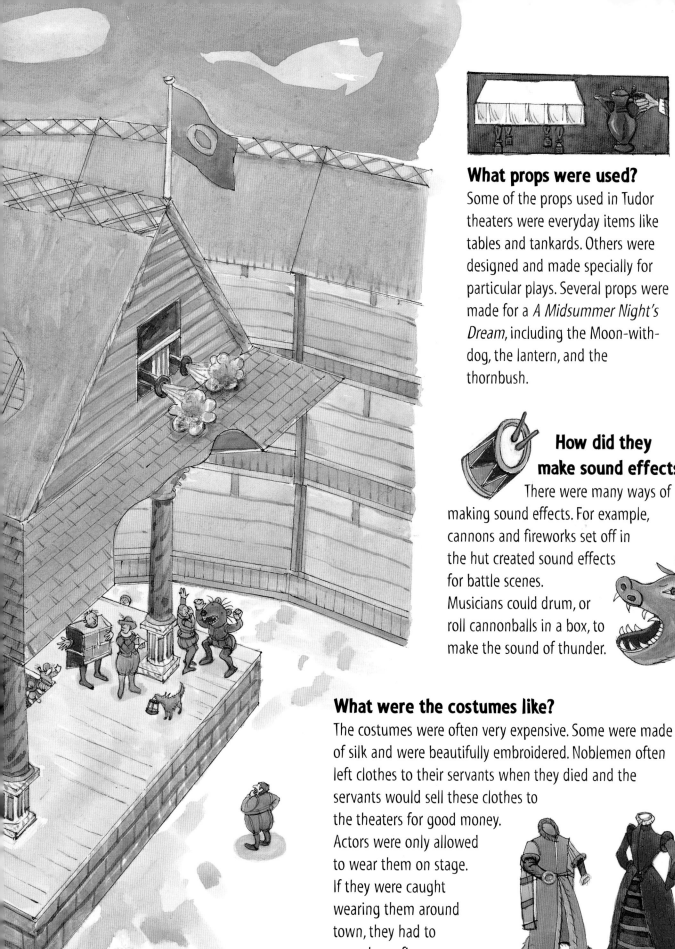

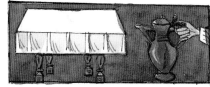

What props were used?

Some of the props used in Tudor theaters were everyday items like tables and tankards. Others were designed and made specially for particular plays. Several props were made for a *A Midsummer Night's Dream*, including the Moon-with-dog, the lantern, and the thornbush.

How did they make sound effects?

There were many ways of making sound effects. For example, cannons and fireworks set off in the hut created sound effects for battle scenes. Musicians could drum, or roll cannonballs in a box, to make the sound of thunder.

What were the costumes like?

The costumes were often very expensive. Some were made of silk and were beautifully embroidered. Noblemen often left clothes to their servants when they died and the servants would sell these clothes to the theaters for good money. Actors were only allowed to wear them on stage. If they were caught wearing them around town, they had to pay a huge fine.

Who went to the theater?

The audience at the Globe was very mixed, very rowdy, and very noisy. But everyone in Tudor London, both rich and poor, loved the new theaters.

People called "hawkers" moved around the theater during the play, selling refreshments. Play-goers could buy bread, ale, pippins (apples), pears, and other tidbits like nuts and gingerbread.

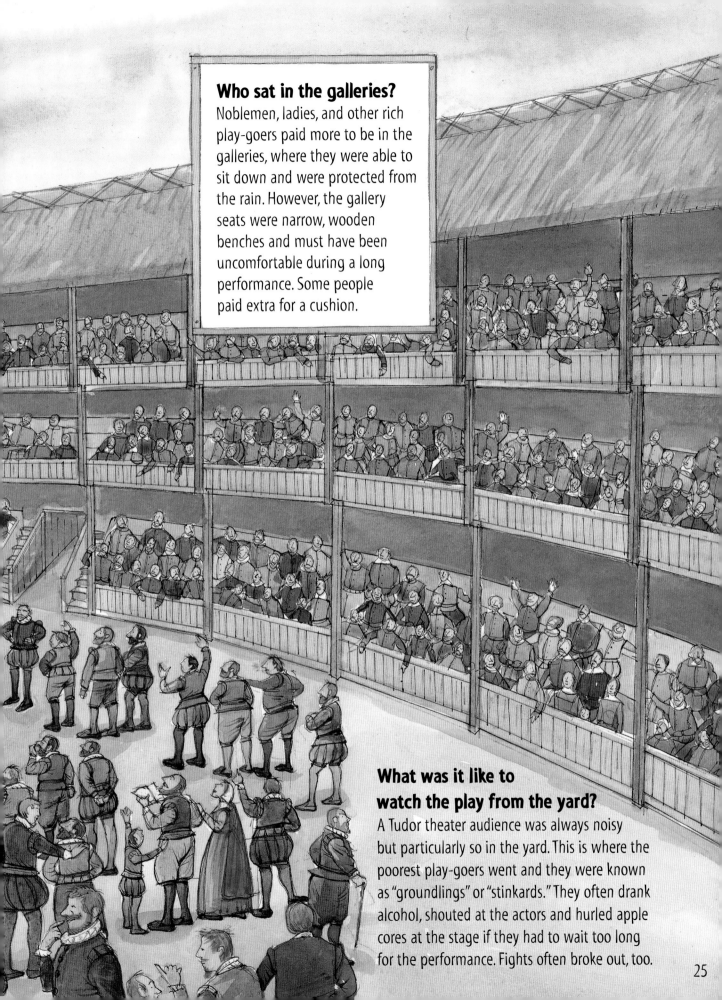

Who sat in the galleries?
Noblemen, ladies, and other rich play-goers paid more to be in the galleries, where they were able to sit down and were protected from the rain. However, the gallery seats were narrow, wooden benches and must have been uncomfortable during a long performance. Some people paid extra for a cushion.

What was it like to watch the play from the yard?
A Tudor theater audience was always noisy but particularly so in the yard. This is where the poorest play-goers went and they were known as "groundlings" or "stinkards." They often drank alcohol, shouted at the actors and hurled apple cores at the stage if they had to wait too long for the performance. Fights often broke out, too.

25

What happened to Tudor theaters?

Very few Tudor theaters lasted more than 20 years. Most of them were made from wood and thatch and were destroyed by fire, or pulled down when theater was banned.

When were theaters banned?

In 1642 some very religious members of Parliament, called Puritans, banned all theaters. A civil war began in England and the king, Charles I, was executed. When his son Charles II came to the throne in 1660, he restored theaters. This period was known as "the Restoration." He even allowed women to act in the new Restoration plays.

King Charles II

a Puritan ▶

Are there Tudor theaters outside of London?

There are Renaissance-style theaters in Italy which are still standing today. The famous Teatro Olimpico amphitheater, in Vicenza, near Venice, was finished in 1584, fifteen years before Shakespeare's Globe. It was Europe's first Classical-style theater. Farther south, in Rome, architects have just built a 21st-century copy of the Tudor Globe and there is another copy in Japan.

◀ Teatro Olimpico, Italy

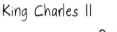

A copy ▶ of the Globe in Rome

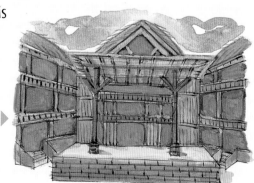

Sam Wanamaker

What remains of Tudor theaters in London?

Today we can see reminders of Tudor theater in London. The American actor Sam Wanamaker began a campaign in 1970. He wanted to build a new Globe theater in London to perform Shakespeare's plays. Twenty-five years later the new Globe opened, close to its original site at Bankside, Southwark, by the Thames River.

Rose Globe

foundations plan of the old Globe

How was the new Globe built?

In 1988 and 1989, the designers of the new Globe had unexpected help. During a building project in Southwark, archeologists found the foundations of the old Globe and Rose theaters.

How else can we remember the Tudor theaters?

We now have "new" Tudor theaters, like the Globe, to remind us of these theaters. But more importantly, perhaps, we can still watch plays that were written 400 years ago, in Tudor times. Many of these plays, and the stories they tell, still have the power to speak to us and entertain us today. They are performed across the world and enjoyed by people of many different cultures.

Othello, from a modern Shakespeare production

Timeline

1564 William Shakespeare is born in Stratford-upon-Avon.

1572 A new law prohibits actors without a noble patron or a license.

1576 James Burbage builds the Theater at Shoreditch, in London.

1587 Philip Henslowe builds the Rose at Southwark, in London.

c.1590 Shakespeare begins to write plays. *The Taming of the Shrew* is one of his earliest.

1592 Shakespeare joins a company of actors to write plays for them to perform.

1593 Christopher Marlowe is murdered in a Deptford inn.

c.1594 Shakespeare's company of actors becomes the Lord Chamberlain's Men. Shakespeare is their leading playwright.

1594 After two years of plague, London theaters are forced to close. Only the Lord Chamberlain's Men and the Lord Admiral's Men survive.

1595-96 Francis Langley builds the Swan theater at Southwark.

1598 The Lord Chamberlain's Men pull down the Theater and use its timbers to build the Globe.

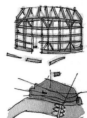

1598 Henslowe builds the square Fortune theater, north of the river.

1603 James I takes the throne. The Lord Chamberlain's Men are renamed the King's Men.

1613 The Globe burns down and is rebuilt.

1614 Henslowe builds the Hope at Southwark.

1616 Shakespeare dies.

1642 Religious Puritans pass an Act of Parliament which closes theaters.

1660 Charles II takes the throne and restores theater to the country.

1970 American actor Sam Wanamaker campaigns to build a copy of the Globe.

1988-9 Archeologists find traces of the sites of the Tudor theaters, the Rose and the Globe.

1995 The first performance at the new Globe theater takes place.

Glossary

balcony
A platform with a rail around it, above the tiring-house, where the actors, musicians and some audience members could sit during a performance.

boy apprentice
Young male actors who played the female characters in plays. Women were not allowed on stage in Tudor times.

gallery
A level of seating around the outside of the theater. Most theaters had three or four galleries.

guild
A group of men in a town or city who shared the same job or craft. The guild made sure its members produced good-quality work.

hawkers
A person who carried around drinks, food, or trinkets to sell in places like theaters and markets.

hut and heavens
An area above the stage used for storing scenery, props, and costumes. The heavens were painted to look like starry skies. They had trapdoors through which actors were lowered to the stage.

masque
A short, dramatic of entertainment performed at court during the 16th and 17th centuries. Masques included dancing, songs, and tableaux.

patron
Someone who gives money to support a charity, a group, or a person.

playwright
A person who writes plays.

Renaissance
The rebirth or rediscovery of the ideas of ancient Greece and Rome, that took place in Europe from the 15th to the 17th century.

tiring-house
A timber-framed building at the back of the stage which was used mainly as a changing room for the actors.

traveling players
Actors who traveled around the country performing shows in public spaces.

winch
A reel or drum used to wind rope up or down. Props or actors could be lowered onto the stage using a winch and a rope.

yard
The audience area in front of the stage. People who bought the cheapest tickets stood in the yard to watch the plays.

Index